P9-DDM-146

LEE COUNTY LIBRARY
107 Hawkins Ave.
Sanford, NC 27330

NIGHT STALKERS SPECIAL OPERATIONS AVIATION

by Andrea L. Weiser

CAPSTONE BOOKS

an imprint of Capstone Press
Mankato, Minnesota

LEE COUNTY LIBRARY
107 Hawkins Ave.
Sanford, NC 27330

Capstone Books are published by Capstone Press
151 Good Counsel Drive, P.O. Box 669, Mankato, Minnesota 56002
http://www.capstone-press.com

Copyright © 2000 Capstone Press. All rights reserved.
No part of this book may be reproduced without written permission from the publisher.
The publisher takes no responsibility for the use of any of the materials or methods
described in this book, nor for the products thereof.
Printed in the United States of America.

Library of Congress Cataloging-in-Publication Data
Weiser, Andrea L.
U.S. Army Special Operations Command: Night Stalkers special operations
aviation/Andrea L. Weiser.
p. cm.—(Warfare and weapons)
Includes bibliographical references and index.
Summary: Introduces the special force of the United States Army known as the
Night Stalkers including their history, training, and equipment.
ISBN 0-7368-0338-6
1. United States Army Special Operations Command. 2. United States.
Army—Aviation—Juvenile literature. 3. Special operations (Military science)
[1. United States Army Special Operations Command. 2. United States. Army—
Aviation. 3. Special operations (Military science)] I. Title. II. Title: US Army
Special Operations Command. III. Series.
UG633.W365 2000
356'.167'0973—dc21
99-21032
CIP

Editorial Credits
Connie R. Colwell, editor; Timothy Halldin, cover designer; Linda Clavel,
    illustrator; Heidi Schoof, photo researcher

Photo Credits
Archive Photos/Ricardo Watson, 16; Philippe Wojazer, 19; Charles Platiau, 21
Corbis-Bettmann, 14
SSG Samuel Armoor/160th Special Operations Aviation Regiment, 27
U.S. Army, 7, 34, 36
Walter Sokalski Jr., cover, 4, 8, 10, 24, 29, 32, 40, 43

**Thanks to the U.S. Army Special Operations Command for assistance on
this book.**

Table of Contents

Chapter 1

Night Stalkers

In 1987, trade ships in the Persian Gulf came under attack. The Persian Gulf is a body of water near the countries of Iraq and Kuwait. The Iraqi government did not want ships from other countries to trade with Kuwait. Iraqi troops tried to destroy trade ships that entered the Persian Gulf.

A specially trained group of U.S. soldiers helped protect the trade ships. At night, the soldiers flew helicopters 30 feet (9 meters) above the water to guard the ships. They used special glasses called Night Vision Goggles (NVGs) to watch for enemy forces in the dark. These night duties earned the soldiers the nickname Night Stalkers.

Night Stalkers wear Night Vision Goggles (NVGs) to help them watch for enemy forces in the dark.

LEE COUNTY LIBRARY
107 Hawkins Ave.
Sanford, NC 27330

Night Stalkers are members of the 160th Special Operations Aviation Regiment (Airborne). The 160th SOAR(A) is a special force of the U.S. Army. Night Stalkers fly helicopters to support other military soldiers.

Special Operations

Night Stalkers are one of the Special Operations Forces. These forces assist the military with dangerous missions. Missions are special military tasks. Other Special Operations Forces include the Army Rangers, the Navy SEALs, and the Air Force Combat Controllers.

The Night Stalkers' main job is to assist the U.S. Army Special Operations Forces. But Night Stalkers also can work with other Special Operations Forces. Together, they can assist soldiers in the U.S. Navy or the U.S. Air Force. Combined, these Special Operations Forces are called joint task forces.

Night Stalkers fly helicopters to support soldiers on the ground.

Night Stalkers

Night Stalkers often perform dangerous missions. They may fly helicopters while enemies shoot at them. They sometimes fly helicopters at low altitudes. Altitude is the height of an object above the ground. Helicopters at low altitudes are easier to shoot at. Night Stalkers also fly their helicopters in poor weather. They perform many of their duties at night and in poor weather.

Night Stalkers on combat missions may use weapons attached to their helicopters.

Night Stalker Missions

Night Stalkers perform three types of missions. They perform combat missions, personnel search and recovery missions, and direct action (DA) missions.

Night Stalkers on combat missions perform various tasks. They often move soldiers and equipment in or out of enemy territory. They drop soldiers safely from helicopters by parachute, rope, or ladder. They carry supplies and equipment to soldiers already on the ground.

Night Stalkers on personnel search and recovery missions use helicopters to rescue pilots. These pilots sometimes crash aircraft in enemy territory. Night Stalkers locate the pilots, rescue them, and bring them to safety.

Night Stalkers on direct action (DA) missions often destroy enemy weapons or bases. Night Stalkers must complete DA missions quickly and accurately. They risk capture or injury on these missions. Night Stalkers use weapons attached to the helicopters to perform DA missions. These weapons may include rockets, missiles, and machine guns.

The Night Stalker Team

The 160th Special Operations Aviation Regiment (Airborne) has four battalions. A battalion is a group of soldiers who train and work together. Each Night Stalker battalion has a fort where the Night Stalkers train and exercise. Three Night Stalker battalions are based at Fort Campbell, Kentucky. The fourth battalion is based at Hunter Army Airfield in

The crew chief controls the guns on the sides of the helicopter.

Georgia. Another small group of Night Stalkers is based at Fort Kobbe in Panama. The Night Stalkers currently have about 1,400 members.

Each Night Stalker helicopter has a crew. These people fly together in the helicopter. Each crew includes a pilot, a copilot, and at least one crew chief.

The Night Stalker pilot flies the helicopter. The pilot controls the helicopter from the cockpit. This control area is located at the front of the helicopter. Each pilot is trained to fly one model of helicopter.

The copilot assists the pilot with control of the helicopter. The copilot sits next to the pilot in the cockpit. The copilot can fly the helicopter if the pilot needs a break or is injured.

The crew chief has various duties. The crew chief controls the guns on the sides of the helicopter. The crew chief checks the helicopter's equipment before a mission. The crew chief loads and unloads equipment and passengers. In the air, the crew chief fixes any problems with the helicopter. The crew chief flies in the same type of helicopter during each mission.

Other Night Stalkers

Other Night Stalkers assist the Night Stalker crewmembers. Each battalion has a flight surgeon. The flight surgeon makes decisions about medical care. Medical assistants called medics help flight surgeons.

Maintenance people care for the helicopters between missions. These Night Stalkers check each helicopter to make sure it is operating properly. They also make necessary repairs.

Human: stands for the Night Stalkers

Moon: shows that Night Stalkers often perform missions at night

Wings: stand for the helicopters that Night Stalkers fly on missions

NIGHT STALKERS

Chapter 2

History of the Night Stalkers

The U.S. military often used helicopters during the Vietnam War (1954–1975). Soldiers used helicopters in many battles. But the soldiers who flew these helicopters were not part of a specially trained group.

Task Force 160
In the 1970s, terrorists began to commit many crimes throughout the world. Terrorists sometimes hold people against their will. These people are called hostages. Terrorists often demand money or favors in exchange for the safety of hostages. Terrorists sometimes injure or kill the hostages.

The U.S. military often used helicopters during the Vietnam War (1954–1975).

15

Manuel Noriega was the leader of Panama during Operation Just Cause.

The army needed a special group to deal with terrorists. In 1981, it created Task Force 160. The members of this force were specially trained to rescue hostages and handle terrorists. They used helicopters to perform these duties. But the members of Task Force 160 did not have a set of rules to help them work together effectively. They were not prepared to perform some dangerous missions.

The 160th SOAR(A)

In 1990, army leaders changed Task Force 160. They made the group part of the U.S. Army Special Operations Command. The Special Operations Command advised the group on how to become more organized. It established guidelines for the Night Stalkers group. These rules and procedures helped the Night Stalkers to better assist in emergency situations. Army leaders named the new group the 160th Special Operations Aviation Regiment (Airborne).

Operation Just Cause

In 1989, George Bush was president of the United States. He ordered U.S. troops into combat in Panama City, Panama. The leader of Panama was Manuel Noriega. Noriega was accused of breaking drug laws. U.S. citizens in Panama were in danger. Other U.S. interests also were threatened.

Night Stalkers gathered 441 soldiers and 46 helicopters from their battalions. Their mission was to capture Noriega and restore order in

Panama. This mission was called Operation Just Cause.

Night Stalker pilots flew soldiers into Panama. Some of these soldiers lowered themselves from the helicopters by rope. Others parachuted to the ground. Enemy gunfire shot down one Night Stalker helicopter. The pilots landed the helicopter in the middle of a street. The pilots and passengers survived the crash. Friendly military forces rescued them.

Operation Just Cause succeeded. U.S. citizens were protected. The Panamanian people had some freedoms restored. U.S. forces later captured Noriega. They put him in jail for breaking drug laws.

Desert Shield and Desert Storm

In 1990, the Iraqi military invaded the country of Kuwait. The United States sent troops to protect Kuwait. The United States and Iraq fought a series of battles. These military operations were called Desert Shield and

The U.S. Armed Forces and its allies drove Iraqi troops out of Kuwait. Night Stalkers helped in this effort.

Desert Storm. These operations also were called the Gulf War (1991).

The 160th SOAR(A) flew the first U.S. helicopters into Iraq during Desert Storm. Night Stalkers used these helicopters to transport U.S. soldiers into Iraq and to destroy Iraqi weapons. Night Stalkers also rescued pilots on the ground. Many of these pilots were from countries friendly with the United States.

All these efforts helped the U.S. Armed Forces and its allies drive Iraqi troops out of Kuwait.

Task Force Ranger

In 1993, the country of Somalia in Africa was in complete disorder. Many people were dying from hunger. The country had several leaders called warlords who were fighting each other. The United States sent Special Operations Forces to Somalia to help restore order. Night Stalkers assisted with these duties. This mission was called Task Force Ranger.

On October 3, 1993, two U.S. helicopters were shot down in Somalia. One U.S. pilot was captured. Night Stalkers used helicopters to rescue the other survivors and protect other U.S. soldiers. Today, Somalia still is not at peace.

Special Operations Forces traveled to Somalia to try to restore order in this country.

Mission

Operation: Urgent Fury

Date: October 25, 1983

Location: The island of Grenada

Mission: Rebels had overthrown the Grenadian government. These rebels were holding U.S. medical students as hostages. U.S. Armed Forces needed soldiers to rescue the students from this island.

U.S. Commandos: Commandos and Night Stalkers traveled to Grenada. Commandos are soldiers specially trained to perform rescue missions on the ground. The Night Stalkers flew over Grenada. But they did not land. The Night Stalkers tried to lower the commandos to the ground with ropes. But the Grenadian rebels fired their weapons at the commandos and helicopters. The Night Stalkers tried several times before they successfully lowered the commandos to the ground.

Rescue: The commandos then found and rescued the hostages. The Night Stalkers had successfully completed their mission.

Kilometers
0 1 2 3

★ Capital

0 1 2
Miles

*Caribbean
Sea*

GRENADA

*Atlantic
Ocean*

★ St. George's

North
America

*Atlantic
Ocean*

*Pacific
Ocean*

South
America

Chapter 3

Training

Men must be army soldiers before they can become Night Stalkers. Women soldiers are not allowed to serve as Night Stalkers. Soldiers who want to be Night Stalkers must complete basic army training. They also must have experience in the army. They then can offer to serve as Night Stalkers.

Night Stalker leaders choose qualified army members for Night Stalker training. Both army soldiers and army pilots can become Night Stalkers. Soldiers can become Night Stalker crewmembers and support people. Pilots can become Night Stalker helicopter pilots. Night Stalker training begins with Green Platoon training. Green Platoon training is different

Soldiers must complete the Green Platoon training course before they can become Night Stalkers.

for soldiers and pilots. This training is difficult. Night Stalker training involves tough physical and mental tests. The training teaches Night Stalkers to be strong and well-prepared.

Green Platoon for Soldiers

The Green Platoon training course for soldiers lasts five weeks. Soldiers learn the history and goals of the 160th SOAR(A) during the first week of training. This helps soldiers understand the Night Stalkers and their duties.

Soldiers learn land navigation skills the second week of Green Platoon. They learn to read and chart maps and use compasses. Navigation skills are useful when Night Stalkers travel in unfamiliar territory.

Soldiers learn about combat during the third week of Green Platoon. They learn how to use Night Stalker equipment in battles. They learn hand-to-hand combat. This type of fighting does not involve weapons. The soldiers also learn to fight with knives.

Soldiers learn survival skills the fourth week of Green Platoon. These skills help them

Soldiers learn survival skills the fourth week of Green Platoon training.

stay alive while on dangerous missions. They learn to survive underwater. They also learn how to save the lives of others.

Soldiers learn to use military weapons during the final week of training. They learn to shoot M-9 pistols and M-4 and M16A2 rifles. Night Stalkers use these weapons to protect themselves and others. Soldiers who complete the five weeks of Green Platoon training can become Night Stalkers.

Green Platoon for Pilots

Pilots spend 14 weeks in Green Platoon training. These soldiers already have worked as pilots in other parts of the army. The training course for pilots is taught in four parts called phases.

In Phase 1, pilots attend Survival, Escape, Resistance, and Evasion (SERE) school. There, pilots learn to survive in unfamiliar territory. They learn to resist enemies. They also learn to avoid danger during missions.

In Phase 2, pilots learn combat skills. They learn skills similar to the skills that soldiers learn. They learn hand-to-hand combat. They learn to use Night Stalker equipment to fight enemies. Pilots also receive special combat training with the U.S. Navy.

In Phase 3, pilots practice flying skills inside helicopters. The pilots do not yet fly helicopters. They first learn to plan safe flights. They learn how to use the equipment inside the helicopters. They also learn to use NVGs to see land and objects in the dark.

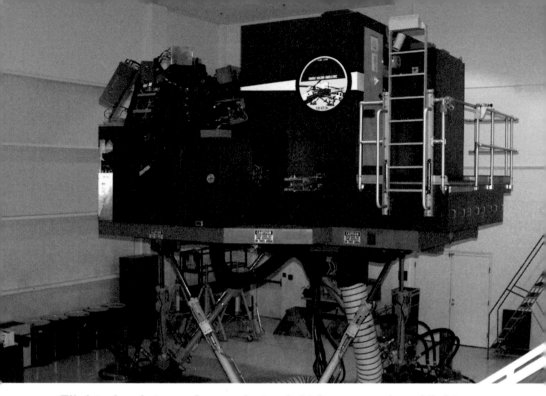

Flight simulators show what might happen when Night Stalkers fly helicopters.

Phase 4 is flight training. Pilots practice for 30 hours in a flight simulator. This computer-controlled machine looks and acts like a helicopter. This part of the training is similar to playing a computer game. The computer shows what might happen when Night Stalkers fly helicopters.

Pilots then fly real helicopters. They fly over all types of land. They learn to use the special equipment in their helicopters. They learn to fly in all weather conditions. They also learn to land helicopters safely.

Pilots who complete this training program are Basic Mission Qualified (BMQ). BMQ pilots can perform some Night Stalker missions.

Advanced Training

Night Stalker pilots can take more training courses after Green Platoon. Two higher training levels are Fully Mission Qualified (FMQ) and flight lead. It takes 12 to 18 months to become FMQ. These Night Stalkers are trained to perform the most difficult Night Stalker missions.

Night Stalkers need another three or four years of training to become flight leads. These Night Stalkers plan missions. Flight leads make all the important decisions about missions.

Military Terms

BMQ – Basic Mission Qualified

DA – Direct Action

FMQ – Fully Mission Qualified

N.S.D.Q! – Night Stalkers Don't Quit!

NVGs – Night Vision Goggles

SERE – Survival, Escape, Resistance, and Evasion

SOAR(A) – Special Operations Aviation Regiment (Airborne)

Chapter 4

Helicopters and Weapons

Night Stalkers need special helicopters to help them perform their missions. These helicopters must be able to fly quickly and for long distances. They must be able to fly at night. Night Stalker helicopters also must be able to refuel in the air.

Night Stalkers use three types of helicopters for their missions. These are light observation, utility, and medium-lift helicopters.

Light Observation Helicopters
Night Stalkers use Little Bird (AH/MH-6) helicopters for direct action (DA) missions.

Night Stalkers need special helicopters like this to help them perform their missions.

33

Little Birds have many features that make them useful for DA missions. Little Birds are small, fast, and easy to fly. They can travel up to 174 miles (280 kilometers) per hour. Little Birds can land in spaces of about 50 feet by 50 feet (15 meters by 15 meters).

Little Birds can go long distances without refueling. These light helicopters can carry two extra fuel tanks. They can travel 400 miles (644 kilometers) without needing more fuel.

Little Birds cannot carry large loads. They can carry a pilot, a copilot, and six passengers. The passengers ride on a platform on the outside of the helicopter. This platform can be folded away when it is not needed.

Utility Helicopters

Night Stalkers often use utility helicopters to perform personnel search and rescue missions. Utility helicopters are large enough to carry both soldiers and equipment. Night Stalkers

Night Stalkers often use Blackhawk helicopters for carrying soldiers and equipment.

Night Stalkers often use Chinook helicopters to carry passengers.

use modified Blackhawk helicopters (MH-60s) for utility missions.

Blackhawk helicopters are large. They move less easily than Little Birds. But Blackhawks can carry more equipment and passengers. These helicopters carry four crewmembers and as many as 12 passengers. Blackhawks can fly a maximum of 222 miles (357 kilometers) per hour. Blackhawks need a larger area to land than Little Birds. Blackhawks need spaces of about 100 feet by 100 feet (30 meters by 30 meters) to land.

Blackhawks carry extra guns and missiles. They also have special weapons attached to them. These helicopters also can be used for combat or to protect other helicopters.

Medium-Lift Helicopters

Night Stalkers use medium-lift helicopters to carry passengers. These helicopters are large and strong. Night Stalkers use Chinooks (MH-47s) as their medium-lift helicopters.

Chinooks can carry many passengers and much equipment. They can carry five crewmembers and 65 passengers. They also can carry heavy loads of equipment. A Chinook can carry a large army truck either inside it or hanging beneath it. Chinooks often carry equipment to Special Operations soldiers on the ground.

Chinooks are sturdy helicopters. Night Stalkers use them for long flights. The normal speed of a Chinook is 137 miles (220 kilometers) per hour. Chinooks can travel as fast as 194 miles (312 kilometers) per hour. Chinooks need an area 100 feet by 150 feet (30 meters by 46 meters) in size to land.

Weapons

Night Stalkers use weapons to protect themselves and others. Some of these weapons are attached to the helicopters. Little Birds and Blackhawks can have guns or other weapons attached to them. The pilot operates these weapons from the cockpit. These guns fire bullets out of the front of the helicopter.

Guns also are attached to the sides of the helicopters. Crew chiefs operate these guns. These side guns fire in fast repetition. They can fire up to 4,000 bullets per minute. They can reach targets as far as 4,920 feet (1,500 meters) away.

Night Stalker helicopters also carry weapons inside. They can carry machine guns, rockets, grenade launchers, and missiles. Soldiers in the helicopters often drop these weapons to soldiers on the ground.

Night Stalkers also carry some weapons on their bodies. They carry M-9 pistols, M-4 rifles, and M16A2 rifles.

Important Dates

1954–1975 – Vietnam War; the U.S. Army begins using helicopters in battle

1981 – U.S. Army creates Task Force 160; the members of this force were specially trained to use helicopters to rescue hostages and handle terrorists

1983 – Operation Urgent Fury; Night Stalkers fly commandos to Grenada; the commandos rescue U.S. citizens from the island

1989 – Operation Just Cause; Night Stalkers help capture Manuel Noriega in Panama

1990 – U.S. Army changes Task Force 160 to SOAR(A); army leaders organize SOAR(A)

1990 – The Gulf War; Night Stalkers fly the first helicopters into Iraq

1993 – Task Force Ranger; Night Stalkers use helicopters to rescue soldiers who crash in Somalia

Chapter 5

The Future

Night Stalkers will continue to perform missions in the future. Advancements in technology will help Night Stalkers on these missions. Night Stalkers will continue to work with other Special Operations Forces.

Technology
Better tools, weapons, and vehicles may help Night Stalkers with future missions. For example, today's crewmembers wear headsets that are hooked to the inside of the helicopters. These headsets help crewmembers communicate with one another. But the headsets also prevent crewmembers from moving around easily. New wireless headsets

Night Stalkers will continue to prepare for future missions.

will make it easier for crewmembers to move more freely.

Today, many Night Stalkers use computers to perform tasks. These tasks had to be performed by hand in the past. Computers help Night Stalkers perform these tasks quickly and accurately.

Sharing Skills

Special Operations Forces will continue to work together on missions in the future. These groups also will begin training together. Joint training will prepare them to perform missions together.

Current members of the 160th SOAR(A) already share their skills with each other. They help train new members. They also help train forces in other countries. Sharing skills and knowledge helps Night Stalkers and other Special Operations Forces successfully perform their missions. Advanced training and new tools will help Night Stalkers complete dangerous missions in the future.

In the future, Special Operations Forces will begin training together.

Words to Know

battalion (buh-TAL-yun)—a large group or unit of people in the armed forces

commando (cah-MAN-doh)—a soldier who is specially trained for difficult missions

evacuation (i-vak-yoo-WAY-shuhn)—the act of removing people from an area

hostage (HOSS-tij)—a person who has been captured and kept as a prisoner

navigation (nav-uh-GAY-shun)—planning and directing a course

regiment (REJ-uh-muhnt)—a unit of troops; each regiment includes at least two battalions.

simulator (SIM-yuh-lay-tur)—a tool used to practice situations; simulators help pilots prepare for real missions.

task force (TASK FORSS)—a combined group of military special forces

To Learn More

Bohrer, David. *America's Special Forces.*
Osceola, Wis.: MBI Publishing, 1998.

Harding, Steve. *U.S. Army Aircraft Since
1947: An Illustrated Reference.* Atglen,
Penn.: Schiffer Publishing, 1997.

Tomajczyk, Stephen F. *U.S. Elite
Counter-Terrorist Forces.* Power
Series. Osceola, Wis.: Motorbooks
International, 1997.

Useful Addresses

U.S. Army Aviation Museum
P.O. Box 620610
Fort Rucker, AL 36362-5134

U.S. Army Special Operations Command
Public Affairs Office
Fort Bragg, NC 28307

Internet Sites

**160th Special Operations Aviation Regiment
     (Airborne)**
http://www.campbell.army.mil/160soar.htm

U.S. Army Aviation Museum
http://www.aviationmuseum.org

Index

LEE COUNTY LIBRARY
107 Hawkins Ave.
Sanford, NC 27330